THE MOST DEMANDED CAREERS

MORE THAN 100 CAREER OPTIONS INCLUDED

NAJEEM PATHAN

I dedicate this book to

My Family

They always stood by me

In all my good and bad times.

Contents

Preface

I met a number of students who came into the pharmacy accidentally when I was pursuing my B. Pharmacy, For example, Jatin was studying for a NEET examination, and he wanted to be a doctor. As a result, he dedicated three years of his life to studying for the NEET, but he was unable to accomplish so and eventually took admission to the BSc Nursing. Another example was Aamir, who wanted to be an engineer, so he took math in 12th grade, but he noticed the growing popularity of pharmacy among students, especially after the Corona outbreak, so he ended up in a pharmacy because of social pressure, current trends, and mob mentality. I am also an example of this; I have always dreamt of being a government officer, but my family insisted that I must become a doctor, so I studied for the NEET examination for two years, but sadly, I ended up in the pharmacy. Samiksha wanted to be a fashion designer, but due to her family's financial difficulties, she enrolled in a BA [political science] program. So these are just a few examples of people who were unable to pursue their desired career due to various factors such as mob mentality, peer pressure, current trends, and so on.

So, the main point is that, due to a lack of knowledge and proper guidance, as well as other factors listed above, we are more likely to pursue careers that we do not desire. To deal with this problem we have come up with this well-written book on career guidance. This book contains information on over 100 career alternatives, as well as unique NEET preparation techniques, interview preparation, and information on several sources for interview preparation.

CHAPTER ONE

Introduction

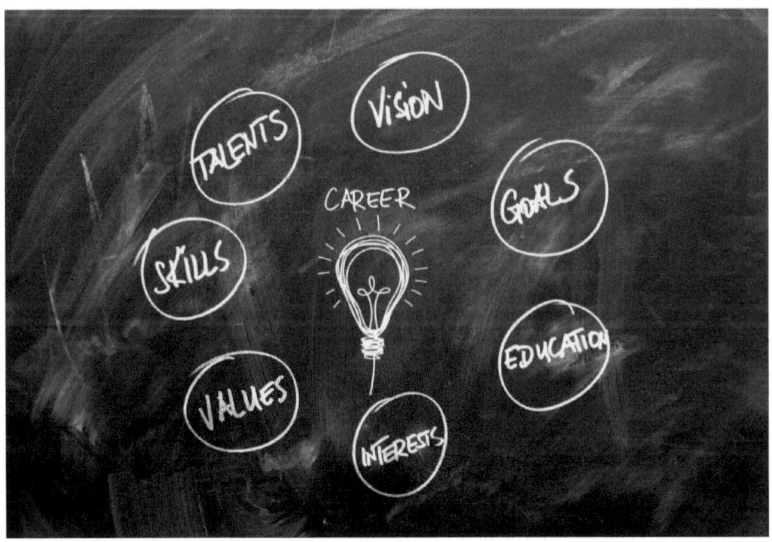

Let me begin with a very elementary question. What is a career? In a general way, a career can be defined as the journey of an individual through work, learning, and other aspects of life. We can say that career is a lifelong process. In which a person goes through professional ups and downs and other stuff. Now some will ask why it is needed to be successful in their career? The answer is very simple, to fulfill our day-to-day, life needs and adds special value to society. So how to choose the right career? In general, we Indians choose our careers based on the following factors.

1. Percentage basis
2. Parental pressure
3. Peer Pressure
4. Mob mentality
5. Financial condition
6. Ongoing trend

These are some factors that decide the career of nearly 70% of Indians. This is only an estimated number, the real numbers may be greater than this. I think you are confused now that, how to make the right choice? The answer is very simple, understand yourself.

Now some of you will ask how to understand ourselves? Again answer is very simple, think about your talents, write down your goals and objectives in life, realize your strength and weaknesses and think that which learning style suits you or the subjects of interest. Just by focusing on these areas, you will be able to understand yourself better than previously. Now take some time to think better and then decide your career path. After all of your research, you're probably ready to make a decision. Based on all of the information you've acquired, choose the occupation that you believe will provide you the most satisfaction. (You're young now. But when you get older and look back at your life, you'll ask yourself a whole bunch of questions. Did I make a difference? Did I contribute something? Did my being here matter? Did I do something that left an imprint?

I'm not asking you to end hunger or repair the ozone. But I am asking you to think about your purpose to recognize that your life isn't infinite and that you should use your limited time here to do something that matters — Daniel H. Pink)

When you know what you want, however, it's much easier to carve out a career path. In the long term, taking these steps early will spare you a lot of pain and confusion.

CHAPTER TWO

Career options after 10th

"What do I do after 10th?" is the biggest and most important question that every kid will face. After the tenth grade, one's professional route can alter one's entire life. To develop a stable and successful profession in the future, you must make a well-thought-out decision. After completing the 10th standard one has mainly three options to take admission in the 11th standard.

1] science 2] commerce 3] arts

1] Science

To take admission in 11th science one has to be good in mathematics, science, and, English. There are mainly the following groupings of subjects available in the science stream

A] Physics, Chemistry, Biology

B] Physics, Chemistry, Mathematics

D] Physics, Chemistry, Mathematics, and Biology

E] Computer science

F] Crop science

Apart from this, there are some other groupings also available like sociology instead of mathematics in the general science group.

Taking admission in the 11th standard with any random elective subject group isn't the sole option. For students who are clear about their objectives, there are numerous options. Diploma classes, short-term courses, army positions, and upper secondary education are all options.

CHAPTER THREE

Medical and Paramedical Courses

"Medical science has proven time and again that when the resources are provided, great progress in the treatment, cure, and prevention of disease can occur." ~ Michael J. Fox

- MBBS
- B.Pharmacy
- BHMS
- D.Pharmacy
- BAMS
- B.Sc Nursing
- BUMS
- DMLT
- BDS
- Occupational Therapy
- Physiotherapy
- BNYS
- Veterinary Science & Animal Husbandry
- Diploma in X-Ray Technology

These are some most popular and the best courses in the medical and paramedical fields. After completing any course you will get a good salary and respect in society.

Now let us discuss in detail some of the most demanded and all-time trending courses.

1] MBBS

Bachelor of Medicine and Bachelor of Surgery is 5.5 Year undergraduate course. The duration of the course is different for different countries. In India first 4.5 years are for academic preparation and the last year is for the compulsory internship. Pharmacology, community medicine, pathology, pediatrics, orthopedics are some subjects taught in the course. One can go for higher education like MD in pathology, MS in orthopedics, master's in hospital management, MSc in clinical pathology, etc.

Admission: So if you want to pursue a Bachelor of Medicine and Bachelor of Surgery you should appear for the NEET exam.NEET is conducted by the National Testing Agency each year. Student must have completed their 12th class with physics, chemistry, biology and they must qualify NEET exam.

Top Colleges: according to the NIRF i.e. National Institute ranking framework the top MBBS colleges are,

1] All India Institute of Medical Sciences, New Delhi.

2] Post Graduate Institute of Medical Education and Research, Chandigarh.

3] Christian Medical College, Vellore, Tamil Nadu.

4] National Institute of Mental Health and Neurosciences, Bengaluru.

5] Sanjay Gandhi Postgraduate Institute of Medical Sciences, Lucknow.

6] Amrita Vishwa Vidyapeetham, Coimbatore.

7] Banaras Hindu University, Varanasi.

8] Jawaharlal Institute of Post-Graduate Medical Education and Research, Puducherry.

9] King Georges Medical University, Lucknow.

10] Kasturba Medical College, Manipal.

Job Opportunities after MBBS:

After completion of the MBBS, you get exposed to a wide range of job opportunities in various organizations both government and private. Let us discuss some of the job opportunities available for MBBS graduates.

There is no doubt that being an MBBS doctor you can open your own clinic or hospital and practice independently. There are several other options such as the medical researcher, medical writer, medical officer in the army, as a faculty in medical college, etc. So after completion of the MBBS, you have so many career options.

2] BDS: Bachelor of dental surgery is a 5-year undergraduate course in which the last one is year is for compulsory internship and the first four years are for academic preparation. General human physiology and biochemistry, Dental materials, General medicine, Oral medicine and radiology, Oral Pathology, and microbiology are some subjects taught in BDS.

Mostly the admission in BDS is done through the NEET exam. There are about 26,950 BDS seats in near about 313 government, private, and deemed institutes of India.

Top colleges: According to the 2021 NIRF Ranking top BDS colleges are,

1] Manipal college of dental sciences, Udupi.

2] Dr.D.Y. Patil Vidyapeeth, Pune.

3] Savitha Institue of Medical and Technical Sciences, Chennai.

4] Maulana Azad Institute of Dental Sciences, Delhi.

5] King Georges Medical University, Lucknow.

6] A.B. Shetty Memorial Institute of Dental Sciences, Mangaluru.

7] Manipal College of Dental Sciences, Manglore.

8] Shri. Ramchandra Institute of Higher Education and Research, Chennai.

9] SDM College of Dental Sciences and Hospital, Dharwad.

10] SRM Dental College, Chennai.

3] BAMS: Bachelor of Ayurvedic Medicine and Surgery is a 5.5-year undergraduate course with internship. Nowadays government of India is promoting Ayurveda under the AYUSH program to provide cost-effective healthcare and promote our traditional medical system. So In upcoming years, BAMS doctors will be in much demand. BAMS doctors can work in Government hospitals, their own clinics, private hospitals, In the domain of clinical research, and many other fields.

Admission: Admission in BAMS is done through the NEET exam. And other exams like KEAM, IPU CET, BVP CET. To take admission in BAMS one must have passed 12th science with a minimum score of 50-60% with PCB group.

Top colleges: According to one of the top educational website ratings here are some of the top colleges of BAMS in India.

1] Banaras Hindu University, Varanasi.

2] Dr. D Y Patil University, Pune.

3] Institute of Medical Sciences, Varanasi.

4] KLE University, Belgaum.

5] Guru Gobind Singh Indraprastha University, New Delhi.

6] DY Patil University, Navi Mumbai.

7] Kurukshetra University, Kurukshetra.

8] Bharati Vidyapeeth Deemed University, Pune.

[note: numbers given in this section to colleges are just for the serial number and not the actual rankings]

Job opportunities after BAMS: BAMS graduates can work in different areas such as clinical research, academics, drug manufacturing, hospital management, and no doubt as a physician. In these areas, BAMS graduates can work on the following job profiles,

Faculty

Clinical research associate

Manger

Physician

Medical writer

The average salary range for all these posts as a fresher may range from 2.5 lakhs to 5 lakhs, it will depend on the organization to organization.

4] B. Pharmacy:

B. Pharmacy is a four-year undergraduate course. The main focus of these four-year studies is on drug manufacturing, dispensing, their adverse action, their mode of action, their physical and chemical aspects, and human anatomy and physiology. In addition to this laws related to the pharmaceutical industry are also included in the syllabus of B. Pharm.

Students of B. Pharm study subjects like Human Anatomy and Physiology, Pharmacology, Medicinal Chemistry, Pharmaceutics, Pharmacognosy, Pharmaceutical Analysis, Pharmaceutical Jurisprudence, Biochemistry, Organic and inorganic Chemistry, Communication skills, etc.

After finishing the B. Pharm course, students can go for higher studies like M. Pharm, MBA, PG Diploma in Clinical Research and Pharmacovigilance, PG Diploma in Forensic Science. Students can also opt for three years LLB course after the B. Pharm, this will open many doors of opportunities for an individual in the field of pharmaceutical industry-related legal matters.

Admission: Admission to the B. Pharm course is done through Different state-level CETs like MHT-CET for Maharashtra state. Apart from this certain ininstitutesstitute, that conduct their own entrance exams like BITSAT are conducted by the Birla Institute of Technology. Students must have scored a minimum of 50% in 12th with Physics, Chemistry, Biology, and mathematics. Students having PCB or PCM group can also be eligible for the course, But they have clear the exam of biology or mathematics before course completion.

Top Colleges: Here are some top colleges, according to the 2021 NIRF Ranking.

1] Jamia Hamdard, New Delhi.

2] Punjab University, Chandigarh.

3] Birla Institute of Technology and Science, Pilani.

4] NIPER, Mohali.

5] Institute of Chemical Technology, Mumbai.

6] NIPER, Hyderabad.

7] JSS College Of Pharmacy, Ooty.

8] Manipal College of Pharmaceutical Sciences, Manipal.

9] JSS College Of Pharmacy, Mysore.

10] NIPER, Ahmedabad.

Job Opportunities after B. Pharm:

B. Forum graduates have ample of opportunities available in many domains. Let us discuss the jobs available after B. Pharm graduation with a realistic salary range.

1] Drug Inspector: Drug Inspector recruitment is done by the UPSC Or other state PSCs like MPSC, KPSC, etc. The first criteria to become is a Bachelor's degree in Pharmacy or Medical sciences like MBBS. Initial Salary for the Drug Inspector may be from monthly 40000 or Above.

2] Clinical Research: In this Domain, there are various job roles like Clinical research associate, clinical research coordinator, clinical data manager, etc. There are many companies, CROs, and Hospitals that provide jobs in this domain. Initial salary may range according to the company or organization you are joining, this may range from 2-3. 5 lakhs per annum.

3] Medical Representative: Medical Representative is a person who informs the doctor about the various medicines to doctors and persuades him to write those medicines on prescription, in short, Medical Representative is the key player of a company in accordance with sales. The average monthly salary range for MR is 20000-35000 for freshers.

4] Core Pharma Industry: We can say that the core pharma industry means where the actual drugs are being manufactured. In this domain, there are job areas like production, quality analysis, quality control, formulation and development, research and development, etc. The average salary will be a little bit less than other domains for freshers but as the experience, you gain it will get an increase.

5] Medical Writer: Medical writer is one of the best careers for pharma graduates. Medical writers work with doctors, scientists, and other subject matter experts, they are responsible for the creation of scientific documents in simple and understandable language. The average monthly salary of a fresher medical writer may range from 20000 to 40000 according to the company or organization.

6] Pharmacovigilance: Now days Pharmacovigilance is gaining tremendous popularity among pharma students. Pharmacovigilance mainly deals with the adverse effect management of drugs. As a fresher one can get an average salary of 19000-35000.

7] Regulatory affairs: This domain is also gaining popularity this day among pharma students. Regulatory affairs mainly deal with drug-related documentation. The average salary in this domain for fresher may range from 22000-38000.

8] Medical Coding: Medical Coders translate long and complicated medical records into simple shortcodes. This is also one of the fastest-growing domains in the healthcare sector. The average salary of the medical coders as a fresher may range from 17000 to 30000.

Apart from this, there are some other domains where you can take your career to a peak level in the healthcare industry. One can also start his own medical shop, medical agency, or small-scale third-party manufacturing company, or other business in the healthcare sector. So if anyone is planning to admission to pharma courses then don't wait just go for it.

5] Bachelor of Veterinary Science and Animal Husbandry {BVSc and AH}: BVSc And AH mainly deal with the treatment and care of Animals and Birds. It is a 5.5-year undergraduate course with an internship. Those students who are from a village background and farmer family have the extra advantage of this course, as farmers have their own animals for various purposes such as farming, milk, and for some extra income. So the students having a farming background will use their this knowledge during the study and it will be easy for them and the other thing is that after completion of the course they can diagnose and treat their animals. Generally, villagers have relationships with surrounding villages so visiting a nearby village and treating their animals will also add extra income. In short, this course has an extra advantage for farming background students.

Applied anatomy, applied nutrition, clinical veterinary medicine, livestock breeding system, principles of animal breeding, and veterinary physiology are some of the subjects taught during the course duration.

Admission: Admission to Bachelor of veterinary sciences and animal husbandry is mainly done through the NEET exam. There might be some other entrance exams depending on the institutes. A student must have passed the exam with a minimum of 50% marks and for reserving the category minimum marks required is 47.50%. Physics, chemistry, biology, or biotechnology with English must be included in their 12th study.

Top Colleges: According to one of the trusted educational websites here are some of the top colleges in India [note: numbering in this section is only for the serial and not the actual ranking of the college]

1] Indian Veterinary Research Institute, Bareilly.

2] Banaras Hindu University, Varanasi.

3] Veterinary College and Research Institute, Chennai.

4] Govind Ballabh Pant University of Agriculture and Technology, Pantnagar.

5] College of Veterinary and Animal Sciences, Bikaner.

6] Birsa Agricultural University, Ranchi.

7] Junagadh Agricultural University, Junagadh.

8] Tamil Nadu Veterinary and Animal Science University, Chennai.

9] Sardar Vallabh Bhai Patel University of Agriculture and Technology, Meerut.

10] West Bengal University of Animal and Fishery Sciences, Kolkata.

Job Opportunities After BVSc and AH:

After passing the BVSc and AH students can do jobs in both government and the private sector, here are some of the most common sectors where BVSc and AH graduates can work.

- Research centers
- Poultry Farms
- Defense dog training centers

- Aviaries
- Government animal husbandry departments
- Animal Breeding Centers
- Agriculture field
- Veterinary Hospitals
- Wildlife sanctuaries

One can work as an Animal Research scientist, veterinary doctor, Livestock development officer, Animal breeder, Veterinary surgeon, etc. The average salary range for all these positions may be 3 to 7 lakhs per annum. The highest salary for a research scientist may be up to 15 lakhs. So you can earn a decent amount of money after completing this course.

These are some of the most popular and the best courses in the medical and paramedical fields. After completing any of the courses above, you will get a good salary and respect in society. So now it will be your decision to choose the course, according to your interest and personality.

CHAPTER FOUR

Engineering and technology courses

"Normal people believe that if it ain't broke, don't fix it. Engineers believe that if it ain't broke, it doesn't have enough features yet." — Scott Adams. Because engineering is such a broad field, there is always room for new ideas and growth. Many things will be said in response to the large number of engineers graduating from Indian colleges, many of whom will be unemployed. Engineering is not for everyone. Basic interest, originality, ingenuity, a high IQ, grasping power, and a willingness to learn from the ground up are all required. Furthermore, they must attend colleges with excellent teaching, infrastructure, and internship opportunities. Now let us have a look at some courses available in Engineering and technology.

- Chemical Technology
- Civil
- Mechanical
- Telecommunication
- Electrical
- Software
- Computer
- Electronics
- Aeronautical
- Marine

- Petrochemical
- Naval Architect
- Biochemical
- Metallurgy
- Biomedical
- Automobile

let us discuss some of the above-mentioned courses in detail,

1] Civil Engineering: Bachelor of engineering [civil] is a four-year undergraduate course. According to Wikipedia civil engineering is considered one of the oldest engineering disciplines. It deals with mainly design, construction, and maintenance of buildings and public work such as canals, dams, roads, etc. Civil engineering may have started between 4000 and 2000 BC in ancient Egypt, Mesopotamia, and Indus valley civilizations. After completion of the bachelor's degree [civil], students can opt for a master's in civil engineering or they can go for MBA or other courses.

Admission: Admission to this course is done through various exams like JEE Mains, JEE Advanced, BITSAT, MHT-CET, and some other institute or state level exams. Students must have studied physics, chemistry, and mathematics in 12th. The minimum percentage criteria for this course is 50% in 12^{th}class. Those students who have done their diploma in any stream of engineering are also eligible.

Top Colleges: According to the NIRF ranking some of the top colleges are;

1] Indian Institute of Technology, Madras.
2] Indian Institute of Technology, Bombay.
3] Indian Institute of Technology, Kharagpur.
4] Indian Institute of Technology, Delhi.
5] Indian Institute of Technology, Kanpur.
6] Indian Institute of Technology, Roorkee.
7] Indian Institute of Technology, Hyderabad.
8] Indian Institute of Technology, Gandhinagar.

9] Indian Institute of Technology, Ropar-Rupnagar.

10] Indian Institute of Technology, Patna.

Job opportunities after Civil Engineering: After completing Civil Engineering there are ample opportunities available in the Public sector, Private sector, and the Government sector also. Let us discuss all three in detail.

A] Public Sector: After the government sector, the public sector is the best for job security and in other aspects as compared to the private sector. There are some PSUs that mean the public sector undertaking these companies either conduct their own exam for hiring or they hire employees based on GATE exams score. Now let us see some examples of PSUs

1] Airports Authority of India [AAI].

2] Hindustan Petroleum Corporation Limited [HPCL].

3] Indian Oil Corporation Limited [IOCL].

4] National Fertilizers Limited [NFL].

5] NLC India Limited [NLC].

6] Nuclear Power Corporation of India Limited [NPCIL].

B] Government Sector: Civil Engineers can work in government sectors in various positions like the IAS, IPS, and IFS conducted by the UPSC as for this post very first criteria is candidate must be a graduate, Hence Civil Engineers can also give UPSC Exam. And the most interesting fact is that percentage of Engineers is increasing among those candidates who clear UPSC. Apart from this, there are job opportunities in,

A] Railways B] CPWD

C] Water Resources D] Military

C] Private Sector: In the private sector, Civil engineers can work on various job roles in Building design and construction, Real estate. On projects of the infrastructure of Highways, Airports, etc. In short, we can say that after completion of civil engineering one can work in construction, planning, and management in the private sector.

So civil engineering is one of the best among all branches of engineering of all time. If you are planning to opt for civil engineering, then just go for it don't think too much, there might be some gossip in society about the engineering fields demand is decreasing day by day but trusts me there is always a chance for highly skilled and bright students. If you are among those who tend to study one day before the exam and score just passing marks during graduation then you will never be going to excel in this field.

2] Computer Engineering: Bachelor of computer engineering is an undergraduate course. It is of total 4 years. Basically, this course deals with the design of computers and computer systems and other related work. During these four years of study, students can learn subjects like operating systems, control systems, computer networks, database management systems, network security, etc. After completion of the bachelor's degree in computer engineering, one can go for the master's in the same or opt for some PG diploma course or management courses like MBA.

Admission: Admissions to this course are mainly done through the JEE exams on all India levels. There are many exams through which you can get admission in this course. MHT- CET is conducted in Maharashtra. WBJEE is conducted by the West Bengal government. And there are some institutes that conduct their own entrance exams for example Birla Institute of technology and Sciences conducts their own entrance exam BITSAT. So you can opt for anyone among them and take admission in your dream college.

Students must have passed 12th with a minimum of 50%. Physics, Chemistry, and Mathematics are compulsory subjects for getting admission in this course.

Top Colleges: According to one of the top-rated educational websites here are some of the top colleges for computer engineering.

1] Indian Institute of Technology, Bombay.

2] Manipal Institute of Technology, Manipal.

3] College of Engineering, Pune.

4] SRM University, Chennai.

5] Vellore Institute of Technology, Vellore.

6] Indian Institute of Technology, Madras.

7] Delhi Technical University, Delhi.

8] Jamia Millia Islamia, New Delhi.

9] Indian Institute of Technology, New Delhi.

10] BMS College of Engineering, Banglore.

These are some of the top colleges, apart from this there are some IITs that are missed mentioning here. There is no doubt that all IITs are excellent in their education. [note- numbers in this section are just serial numbers and not the actual ranking of the colleges.]

Job opportunities after computer Engineering: After completion of the bachelor's degree in computer engineering wide range of job opportunities opens for students in various sectors. The job profiles for computer engineers are project engineer, web developer, software developer, back end operator, Research scientist, software tester, front end developer, IT support analyst, IT consultants, Assistant professor, etc. People who are interested in government jobs can join the government organizations like ISRO, NRSC i.e. National Remote Sensing center, etc. MNCs like Microsoft, Facebook, google, amazon, etc hire computer engineers. Apart from MNCs, there are some corporate houses, banks, software development companies, and web designing firms that offer the job for computer engineers. The average salary range for computer engineers is 3 to 7 lakhs per annum it may vary according to the company and the job profile.

3] Aeronautical Engineering: Aeronautical Engineering is one of the most demanded branches of engineering. It mainly deals with the design, construction, and maintenance of aircraft and their various components. There are handful of institutes that offers aeronautical engineering course. In India majority of the colleges offers aerospace engineering which is quite similar to aeronautical engineering. Flight dynamics, aircraft structures, engineering graphics, control engineering, aircraft design project, and solid mechanics, are some subjects taught in Aeronautical engineering.

Admission: Students must have secured at least 70-75% in 12th standard with physics, chemistry, and mathematics. JEE mains and the advanced score is accepted for admission in Aeronautical Engineering.

TopColleges: According to one of the educational websites here are some of the top colleges of Aeronautical Engineering. [note: numbering in this section denotes only serial numbers and not the actual ranking of the colleges]

1] Indian Institute of the Space Science and Technology, Thiruvananthapuram.

2] Indian Institute of Technology, Bombay.

3] Indian Institute of Technology, Kanpur.

4] Manipal Institute of Technology, Manipal.

5] Sathyabama Institute of Science and Technology, Chennai.

6] Indian Institute of Aeronautical Engineering, Dehradun.

7] Hindustan Institute of Technology and Science, Chennai.

8] Nitte Meenakshi Institute of Technology, Banglore.

9] Kumaraguru College of Technology, Coimbatore.

10] Acharya Institute of Technology, Banglore.

Job Opportunities after Aeronautical Engineering:

Aeronautical engineers can work in various areas like aircraft manufacturing companies, defense services, aeronautical laboratories, research centers like NASA, ISRO, defense research and development organization[DRDO], Hindustan aeronautics limited, gas turbine research establishment[GTRE] commercial airlines like Air India, Spicejet, IndiGo, drone design. So if you have completed Aeronautical Engineering and you are highly skilled then the sky will be your limit.

CHAPTER FIVE

Other courses

"At the end of the day, you are solely responsible for your success and your failure. And the sooner you realize that you accept that, and integrate that into your work ethic, you will start being successful. As long as you blame others for the reason you aren't where you want to be, you will always be a failure." — Erin Cummings. So, unfortunately, you didn't get admitted to one of the engineering or medical courses. Then don't worry here are some of the courses apart from medical, paramedical, Engineering, and technology. So let's have a look at them.

1. B. Sc Agriculture
2. Bachelor of Fisheries Science
3. BCA
4. B. Sc Horticulture
5. B. Sc in Biotechnology
6. B. Arch
7. B. Source in Bioinformatics
8. B. Sc IT
9. B. Sc Forensic Science
10. General B. sc

1] BSc Agriculture: BSc Agriculture is an undergraduate course, which is of a total of 4 years. This four years syllabus is framed in such a way that students would get familiar with plant breeding genetics, agricultural microbiology, soil science, etc. Also, students get familiar with the implementation of the latest agricultural techniques and agricultural equipment. So if you are from a farming background definitely you will get extra benefits.

Admission: In Maharashtra admission to this course is mainly done through the MHT-CET which is conducted by the Maharashtra government's Directorate of technical education and also through ICAR AIEEA which national-level exam conducted by the national testing agency. Students must have completed 12th science with either PCMB or PCB group and have scored a minimum of the 55%.

Top colleges: Under the Indian council of Educational Research there are three central agricultural universities, four deemed universities, and sixty-three state agricultural universities. Among these according to one of the top-rated educational websites here are some of the top agricultural colleges. [note: numbering in this section denotes only serial numbers and not the actual ranking of the colleges]

1] Tamilnadu Agricultural University, Coimbatore

2] Acharya NG Ranga Agricultural University, Guntur

3] Punjab Agricultural University, Ludhiana

4] Anbil Dharmalingam Agricultural College and Research Institute, Tiruchirappalli

5] Govind Ballabh Pant University of Technology and Agriculture, Pant Nagar

6] Mahatma Phule Krishi Vidyapeeth, Pune

7] Birsa Agricultural University, Ranchi

8] Dr. Rajendra Prasad Central Agricultural University, Samastipur

9] Junagadh Agricultural University, Junagadh

10] Dr. Balasaheb Sawant Kokan Krishi Vidyapeeth, Ratnagiri

Job Opportunities after BSc Agriculture:

Indian economy is agriculture dominated, hence there are ample job opportunities available in various sectors like, banking, seed manufacturing companies, MNCs, central and state government departments, fertilizer manufacturing firms, food processing units, government research institutes, agricultural universities, etc in this sector one can work on job titles like ICAR scientist, marketing executive, research fellow, agricultural officer, plant breeder, seed technologist, project associate, etc.

The average salary range for freshers may range from 3.5 lakh to 10 lakhs. Salary depends on the candidate's skills and knowledge and also on the company and job profile. So if you are already doing this course and want to apply for a job, I want to give you one piece of advice; please focus on communication skills, be confident, and try to learn new skills. And remember that [Clarity precedes mastery and it's impossible to create an outcome/goal/result that you can't even see] – from the book of Robin Sharma

2] BSc Forensic Science: BSc forensic science is an undergraduate course of a total of 3 years duration. This course mainly covers all the scientific knowledge used in the investigation of crime-related cases. It includes analysis of the bloodstains, fingerprints, recovery of data from laptops, mobiles, computers, and DNA profiling. If you have strong analytical skills, technical skills, observational skills, able to work for long hours, and a keen interest in forensic science, then in my opinion you should go for this course for a bright and satisfying career.

Here are some subjects you can learn during the three years period of this course, introduction to criminology, criminal behavior, introduction to forensic science, analysis of biological fluids, introduction to toxicology, personal identification, DNA fingerprinting, etc.

Admission: Admission to this course is mainly done through the AIFSET. Some institutes offer admission through their own entrance exams and some institutes accept only board percentages. The basic eligibility for this course is that the student must have completed 12th science with a minimum of 50%.

Job opportunities after BSc Forensic science:

Students who have successfully completed this course can work in both private and government sectors such as CBI- central bureau of investigation, IB – Intelligence bureau, forensic science laboratories, clinical research, civil services, etc. in these departments they can work as; police officer, forensic expert, forensic scientist, forensic toxicologist, forensic engineer, forensic architect, crime laboratory analyst, forensic consultant, etc.

The average salary for freshers may range from 2.5 lakhs to 7 lakhs per annum this can go up with the experience and skills you have acquired. One of the great personalities of all time said that if you set your goals ridiculously high and its failure, you will fail above everyone else's success.

3] Bachelor of Fisheries science: BFSc is four years undergraduate course in which you can learn about fisheries environment and fisheries extension, study and investigation of fish processing, aquaculture, and fishery resource management in short this course deals with processing, managing, marketing, and conservation of fishes.

Here are some of the subjects you can learn during the four years of study; principles of aquaculture, fundamentals of microbiology, fishery economics, the culture of fish food organisms, aquaculture engineering, disaster management in fisheries, fishery genetics and breeding, etc.

Admission: Students must have passed the 10+2 with physics, chemistry, and biology. Some institutes provide admission directly on the basis of the percentage of the 12th standard. Some institutes gave admission through ICAR common entrance exam. There are also some institutes that conduct their entrance exam.

Top Colleges: according to one of the top educational websites here are some of the top colleges for BFSc. [note: numberings in this section are only for serial numbers and not the actual ranking of the colleges]

1] Govind Ballabh Pant University of Technology and Agriculture, Pant Nagar

2] Annamalai University, Chidambaram

3] Birsa Agricultural University, Ranchi

4] Mahatma Jyoti Rao Phoole University, Jaipur

5] Dr. Rajendra Prasad Central Agricultural University, Samastipur

6] Junagadh Agricultural University, Junagadh

7] Vasant Rao Naik Marathwada Krishi Vidyapeeth, Parbhani

8] Dr. Balasaheb Sawant Konkan Krishi Vidyapeeth, Ratnagiri

9] West Bengal University of Animal and Fishery Sciences, Kolkata

10] Kerala, University of Fisheries and Ocean Studies, Panagad, Kochi.

Job Opportunities after BFSc:

After completing a bachelor of fisheries sciences one can get numerous job opportunities in both government and private sector. Job titles can be fisheries officer, fishery technician, fishery observer, fisheries biologist, fishery manager, assistant fisheries development officer, district fisheries development officer, etc following government agencies recruit the candidate as technical officers or assistant directors;

- Marine product export development authority
- Export inspection agency
- Fisheries survey of India
- Coastal aquaculture authority of India
- National institute of oceanography
- Food safety and standards authority of India
- Indian national center for ocean and information services

The salary for freshers may vary from 2.5 lacs to 3.5 lacs per annum depending on your knowledge and skills.

4] Bachelor of Computer Application[BCA]: Bachelor of computer application is three years undergraduate course mainly focuses on computer application and software development. BCA is considered equivalent to B.Tech so the benefit of doing BCA is that you can work as a software developer, or system engineer, on other hand B.Tech graduates also work on the same position. The duration of the B.Tech course is 4 years and fees is also higher than BCA, so you can be a software developer or system engineer

After completing BCA in 3 years and paying less fees than B.Tech. So these are the major benefits of doing a bachelor of computer application. If you can spend hours in front of a laptop or PC and have a keen interest in technology, in my opinion, you must do this course. Another reason for opting for this course is that today's world is going towards fully automated things and technology plays a key role in this. So upcoming in years all things will be dominated by technology hence doing BCA will open a pool of job opportunities in every sector.

Admission: One can take admission in bachelor of a computer application on the basis of marks obtained in 12th standard. Minimum 50% marks required for admission in bachelor of computer application. There are [approximately]400 BCA colleges in Maharashtra. Some colleges conduct their own entrance exam for admission and some colleges offer admission on a percentage basis.

Job opportunities after BCA:

Candidates with having a bachelor of computer application can work in both government and private sectors. In top IT companies, you can work as Software Developer, Technical Support, IT Analyst, Web Developer, Junior Analyst, Computer Support Service Specialist, Software Publisher, or you can prepare for government exams like SSC CGL, BHEL, Bank exams, UPSC, SSC, Railway Exams, etc.

There is one job profile called cyber security professional after completing BCA and doing some short-term cyber security courses you can work on this job profile. And the average salary for this is about 5 to 12 lakhs per annum.

Another one is blockchain development, if you want to pursue a career in this domain then you have to do some online or offline courses in blockchain development. Generally, the salary of blockchain developers is over 5.5 lakhs per annum.

So if you are thinking to take admission in a bachelor of computer application and you have a keen interest in learning new technologies then don't waste your time just go for it.

CHAPTER SIX

Arts

Students doing a bachelor's degree in arts have good chances of getting selected in civil services or other government exams because a major portion of the syllabus of bachelor of arts and civil services exams is similar. So if you are pursuing BA you have one good option of preparing for civil exams.

Another thing is that after doing a master's in subjects like economics, political science, history, geography, English literature, etc you can work as an assistant professor or can work as a historian, political scientist, philosopher, etc.

Here are some of the subjects in which you can do an honors degree or your master's.

1. Political science
2. Geography
3. History
4. Economics
5. English literature
6. Sociology
7. Hindi literature
8. Anthropology
9. Psychology
10. Actuarial Science

Philosophy

Rural Development Students can get jobs after completing BA graduation with ease. With options ranging from Psychology, Anthropology, History, Literature, Political Science, Philosophy,

Foreign languages, Foreign Studies, Tourism, Public Relations, Sociology, and more, a student can easily plan his or her Bachelor of Arts course for his or her future aims.

The BA scope of work for a graduate is broad and covers a wide range of professions and industries. Following are some of the most common careers that graduates pursue after completing their BA:

a. Executive Assistant
b. Operations Manager
c. Human Resources Manager
d. Graphic Designer
e. Content Writer
f. Operations Team Leader
g. Marketing Manager
h. Business Development Manager

Graduates with a BA can find employment in both the commercial and public sectors. Students completing a BA course are not limited to their specific disciplines after graduation, resulting in a wide range of professional opportunities. The BA program is an all-around program with various specialties.

Some of the areas of recruitment are:

a. Advertising
b. Law
c. Broadcast
d. Library and Information Science
e. Business Process Outsourcing Units
f. Policing
g. Civil Services
h. Professional Writing
i. Community Service
j. Religious Studies
k. International Relations
l. Social Work
m. Journalism and Mass Communication

CHAPTER SEVEN

Commerce

According to Paul S. Lomax, "Commercial education is fundamentally a program of economic education that has to do with the acquirement, conservation, and spending of wealth".

To achieve a region's or country's financial growth, professional economists and accountants with significant practical knowledge are required to examine and analyze the nuances of large-scale business and others. In India, commerce is originally chosen as an academic discipline at the intermediate level, or after class 10th. At the undergraduate level, a B.Com. can be acquired by studying a range of courses. A basic degree or a specialist degree are also options. A certain subject as a major in order to obtain a B.Com.(Hons). For instance, if a candidate wishes to pursue Accountancy as a career, Bachelor's degree in hand, then B.Com. The degree of (Hons.) in Accountancy is conferred.

Graduates of commerce can choose from a variety of jobs. They have the ability to serve in a range of roles. People from all walks of life contribute to the role of finance and accounting in society. Every person's and company's daily existence are intertwined. Here are some of the most demanded career options;

Chartered Accountant

One of the most popular courses among commerce students is Chartered Accountancy. For students who excel in accounting and finance, Chartered Accountancy is a viable alternative. Chartered accountant positions are available in a variety of sectors, including finance, tax administration, auditing, financial analysis, cost analysis, and consultancy. The average salary range for CA is 7 lakhs per annum, and there is no limit to the salary for skilled and experienced CA.

Company Secretary

The position of company secretary is one of the most senior in the organization. The efficient administration of a company is the responsibility of the company secretary. Students who excel at business studies and management theories may benefit from this course.

Finance Analyst

One of the most in-demand jobs in the financial business is that of a financial analyst. In order to help a firm grow, a financial analyst does macroeconomic and microeconomic research and collects financial data as well as corporate fundamentals.

Portfolio Manager

According to Wikipedia "A Portfolio Manager is a professional responsible for making investment decisions and carrying out investment activities on behalf of vested individuals or institutions.

CHAPTER EIGHT

Home Science

Home Science, also known as Home Economics, is the study of the relationships that exist between people, families, communities, and the environment. We can say that It is the art of managing a home and other resources. It educates how to use science and the humanities to better family nutrition, human environment, resource management, and the development of children. Fabric & Apparel Sciences, Resource Management, Communication & Extension, Nutrition & Food, and Human Development are the five main streams from which students can choose courses.

1. BSc in Home Science
2. Diploma in Home Science
3. MA in Home Economics
4. MSc in Home Science
5. BEd in Home Economics
6. MSc Food Science and Biotechnology
7. MSc in Nutrition and Food Science
8. MSc in Nutrition Science
9. Master of Food Science and Technology
10. Post Graduate Diploma in Home Economics
11. Postgraduate Certificate in Education in Home Economics
12. Ph.D. in Home Economics

Job Opportunities

There are several job opportunities available in both the public and commercial sectors once students have completed their education. Government mess, restaurants, cafeterias, community centers, hospitals, welfare organizations, counseling, educational institutes, fashion journalism, clothes merchandising, and other sectors of employment are among the most common. Here are some of the most common job titles for Home Economics graduates:

1. Dietician
2. Demonstrator
3. Research Scientist
4. Nutritionist
5. Assistant Dietician
6. Food Analyst
7. Counselor, Professor, and Researcher
8. Hostess and Receptionist
9. Health and Nutrition Journalist

The average salary per annum may vary from 2.5 lakhs to 5 lakhs according to job role and organization.

CHAPTER NINE

Talent Based Careers

You know you're a creative person when...

Original music is playing in your head. When taking down notes at a work meeting, you sketch cartoons or drawings. When you act out scenes from your favorite films, people applaud you. If you had ever wished to use your artistic abilities to make a living? Make use of your wonderful voice as a radio announcer. In advertising or marketing communications, you can write your way to fame and money. Think about working as a web designer. It might be difficult for artistic and creative persons to find jobs that suit them. It's easy to feel trapped by typical professions when you're used to thinking outside the box. It's a good thing the world of work is diverse enough to require your multiple skills.

Here are some examples of creative jobs where you can build a fantastic and satisfying career:

1. Radio Jockey
2. News Reporter
3. Choreographer
4. Singer
5. Music Composer
6. Make-up Artist
7. Actor
8. Pet Grooming
9. Hair Stylist
10. Sport Based career
11. Photographer

12. Graphics Designer
14. Writer
15, Poet

CHAPTER TEN

Hospitality Industry careers

The hospitality industry encompasses lodging, food and beverage service, event planning, theme parks, travel, and tourism. It consists of hotels, travel agencies, restaurants, and bars. The world around us is obviously in a state of change. This is particularly true in the hospitality industry. The industry has grown tremendously throughout the years. Many positions in the hospitality business need face-to-face interaction with consumers in a variety of ways. However, there are other careers in sales, marketing, and accountancy that are hidden behind the scenes. Food service employment, such as wait staff and food preparation, abound in the hospitality business.

A list of some of the most prevalent job titles in the hospitality sector follows.

1. Concierge
2. Event Planner
3. Executive chef
4. Hotel Manager
5. Waiter
6. Front Office Manager
7. Tour Guide

Because the hotel business is so diversified, persons seeking hospitality jobs can choose from a wide range of job opportunities. It is critical to understand the various possibilities available whether you want to work in food and beverage service, a front office position, cleaning and maintenance, or as a manager.

CHAPTER ELEVEN

Post Covid career Options

The Covid-19 virus impacted negatively on a variety of sectors. As a result, we must now shift our focus to alternative professional paths which are still viable. We've seen employment markets grind to a halt as people are forced to stay indoors due to lockdowns and social isolation. Professionals must now step up their game in order to anticipate more work prospects or other career paths in the post-pandemic era. The following are a few areas that are expected to grow in popularity in the near future. Here are five alternative career paths to consider in the post-Covid era.

1. Online teaching
2. Cybersecurity careers
3. Freelancing
4. Digital Marketing
5. Social media Influencers

So, if you want to survive this situation, it's time to brush up on your skills. Some industries, such as the ones stated above, will undoubtedly thrive during the current recession and will likely generate more jobs in the future.

CHAPTER TWELVE

Skill Based In Demand careers

The job market has always evolved, and technology-driven jobs are getting increasingly popular. Having specific career skills might boost your chances of success no matter what field you choose. You'll need to study in-demand skills to advance your profession and set yourself apart from other prospects. Here are some of the most in-demand abilities you should work on to help you stay a competitive job prospect.

1. UI/UX design
2. Blockchain
3. Cloud computing
4. IOT
5. Robotic process automation
6. SEO marketing
7. Machine learning
8. Data visualization
9. Mobile App development
10. Artificial intelligence

Because they're at the leading edge of innovation, these skills are in high demand."

CHAPTER THIRTEEN

Competitive Exams

Whether it's jobs, schools, or further education, India is a competitive place. A student can appear for a variety of competitive exams. Furthermore, these competitive exams are divided into mainly three groups: competitive exams after 12th standard, competitive exams after graduation, and examinations for jobs. For government posts, there are a number of competitive exams in India. Competitive exams, are generally conducted to determine a candidate's eligibility. Candidates are evaluated based on their grades and percentile scores. The prime objective of these competitive examinations is to identify deserving individuals without bias. Furthermore, individuals select competitive tests for subsequent studies after 12th or after graduation and opt for government positions to discover the ideal profession.

Competitive exams are difficult since there are many candidates competing for a fixed number of seats. Bank tests, defense examinations, insurance examinations, railway exams, staff selection commission exams, research exams, UGC exams, and UPSC are the most common competitive exams in India.

Here are some of the competitive exams.

1. UPSC
2. Staff selection commission
3. Combined defense service examination
4. NDA examination
5. IBPS PO
6. JEE

7. NEET
8. GATE
9. NET
10. CAT
11. State PSCs

UPSC

The Civil Services Examination is a national-level competitive exam. It is one of the toughest civil services exams, including the Indian Administrative Service. It is conducted by the Union Public Service Commission (UPSC). UPSC exam is conducted mainly in three stages, Preliminary exam, mains exam and interview. Candidates who pass this tests are assigned to various positions, including IAS, IRS, IPS, IFS, and others.

A Bachelor's Degree in any discipline from a recognized university or the Central Government of India is required. Candidates in their last year or who are taking their final semester are also eligible to apply. The candidates' minimum and maximum ages must be 21 and 32 years old, respectively. Candidates in the SC and ST categories would get a 5-year upper age relaxation, while those in the OBC category will have a 3-year higher age relaxation. Success in UPSC is dependent on a one- or two-year period of dedicated preparation with a well-defined strategy.

Staff Selection Commission

The Staff Selection Commission is the conducting body in charge of recruiting personnel for India's many Ministries and Departments. SSC Exams, such as SSC Stenographer, SSC GD, SSD JHT, SSC CGHL, SSC CGL, SSC MST, SSC JE, and others, are held every year for this purpose by the Staff Selection Commission to select various staff in India's multiple departments, ministries, and organizations. SSC exam is one of India's most competitive examinations, with lakhs of people attempting it each year and thousands of positions available. The level of competition for SSC Online tests is relatively high, so SSC Exam preparation should be done ahead of time if you want to pass the exam.

List of the examinations conducted by the SSC;

1. SSC CGL (Combined Graduate Level)
2. SSC MTS (Multi Tasking Staff)
3. SSC CHSL (Commission Combined Higher Secondary Level)
4. SSC JHT (Junior Hindi Translator)
5. SSC CPO (Central Police Organization)
6. SSC JE (Junior Engineer)
7. SSC GD (General Duty)
8. SSC Stenographer
9. SSC Scientific Assistant

NDA Examination

UPSC organizes the NDA exam for entry to the Army, Navy, and Air Force wings of the NDA. This exam provides a pathway for those interested in joining the Army, Navy, or Air Force. NDA is a national-level exam held twice a year to help students in pursuing a career in the military.

Criteria for Eligibility

Physical Requirements

For admission to the National Defence Academy (NDA) and Naval Academy (NA) Examinations (I) and (II), candidates must be physically and mentally fit. Every year, a large number of candidates fail the medical exam. As a result, candidates are urged to have a medical assessment before applying for the exam. Wax (ears), Deviated Nasal Septum, Hydrocele/Phimosis, Overweight/ Underweight, Under Sized Chest, Piles, Tonsillitis, and Varicocele are among the minor defects/ailments that aspirants should address.

Aspiring candidates should maintain good physical health by following the program outlined below. 1. jogging In 15 minutes, you'll have covered 2.4 kilometers. 2. Ignoring 3. Sit-ups and push-ups (minimum 20 each) Chin-ups are a type of chin-up exercise (minimum 08) 5. Climbing a rope that is 3-4 meters long.

Educational qualification

1. For the Army Wing of the National Defence Academy, candidates must have completed Class 12 of the 10+2 school system or an equivalent examination administered by a State Education

Board or a University.

2. For the Air Force and Naval Wings of the National Defence Academy, as well as the 10+2 Cadet Entry Scheme at the Indian Naval Academy, candidates must have a Class 12 pass or equivalent in Physics and Mathematics conducted by a State Education Board or a University.

CHAPTER FOURTEEN

Interview Tips

1. Make an effort to look your best throughout the interview. Your appearance should show that you are serious about the interview. Do not attempt to attend the interview in an unsuitable manner. Some grooming fundamentals will be beneficial.

a. Well Groomed Hair

b. Well Pressed Shirt

c. Polished Shoes

2. Give a direct and concise answer. Make your points as clear as possible. Also, attempt to back up your point with examples. Don't use a lot of words and try to make your responses short and sweet.

3. Be professional and present your views. If you disagree with something expressed by the Interviewer, don't dismiss it as invalid. Even if their viewpoint differed from yours, learn to appreciate it. This isn't to say that you have to agree with what they're saying.

4. The majority of interviewers will give you the opportunity to ask questions. Make the most of this opportunity to demonstrate your knowledge of and interest in the firm. This is also an excellent time to clear up any lingering doubts.

5. Be confident and speak softly.

Here are some websites that can help you.

1. Glassdoor
2. Ambitionbox
3. Quora
4. Geeksforgeeks
5. Indiabix

6. Freshersworld
7. Codercareer

When looking for a job, your resume is your most crucial tool. It doesn't matter how qualified you are or how much expertise you have; if your resume is poorly presented or written, you will have a difficult time landing the job you desire - or even receiving an interview.

Here are some of the websites which will help you build a best resume.

1. CVmaker
2. Resume Genius
3. Resume builder
4. Resume Baking
5. VisualCV

We've covered nearly all of the most popular career paths. However, if you still have any questions or concerns about your career, our specialists are available at 7028212717. We will be happy to assist you.

Printed by Libri Plureos GmbH in Hamburg,
Germany